Is There a Creator?

Why It Matters What You Believe!

By

Otto Engelberth

Copyright © 2011 Otto Engelberth

ISBN 978-1-60910-759-8

All rights reserved. No part of this publication may be reproduced, stored in a retrieval system, or transmitted in any form or by any means, electronic, mechanical, recording or otherwise, without the prior written permission of the author.

Printed in the United States of America.

BookLocker.com, Inc.
2011

First Edition

Dedication

Initially, when sitting at the keyboard writing this book, I visualized my audience to be my grandchildren and great grandchildren. As time went on, my vision expanded to include all of you who were looking over my shoulder as I typed. I envisioned the questions that were on your mind - questions that drove the subject matter of this book.
It is to you that I dedicate this book.

Contents

FORWARD	**ix**
INTRODUCTION: There is a war going on.	**1**
PART I: Our Mind's Logic Points Us to a Creator	**3**
Paradigm; everybody has one.	3
Why most people believe there is a Creator.	4
The human dimension of time.	4
The law of "cause and effect" begs for an answer.	5
Our human curiosity asks what drives the order and complexity of the universe.	5
Our human need to have a context for our existence.	5
Unanswered questions.	6
PART II: The Bible's Description of the Creator	**9**
What do we know about the Creator?	9
The Creator, from the Bible's perspective.	10
Characteristics of the Creator.	11
PART III: The Bible's Description of the Creation Process	**13**
Angels.	13
The Old Testament account of physical creation.	14
The Garden of Eden.	16
The Creator's plan for reconciling man to Himself and reestablishing man's Creator given earthly domain.	17
PART IV: The Creator Wants Us to Believe Him	**20**
Gospel of John Chapter 3: Verses 1 thru 22 from the Living Bible	20
With God it's always been about Belief.	22
Abraham believed God.	23

Moses believed God...24
However, even with God's presence among them, most Israelites did not believe God. 25

PART V: Why is it So Difficult for Man to Believe God?...26

We want to hang on to the illusion that we are in control. ...26
Belief and its counterfeits. 28
Belief is difficult for us because of how our mind works.....29
The role that emotions play in our believing God. 33
God's Holy Spirit enables man to believe in Him. 34

PART VI: Being Spiritually Reborn into God's Family 37

What happens when we are spiritually born again?..............37
God's relationship with us. 38
Jesus' central role in the Kingdom..39
The consequences of unbelief. 41

PART VII: Successful "Kingdom Living"............................42

God's priority..42
Words matter in God's Kingdom...43
We need to learn God's word for our mental health.............44
Having a relationship with God. 45
Jesus lets us use His name. 49
Our character and actions say a lot about our relationship with God..50
Love helps us avoid the "School of Hard Knocks." 51
Our vision drives our choices. 53
God's purpose drives our God-given vision. 56
The context of our God given vision. 58

PART VIII: The benefits of believing God............................61

The Bible gives the believer insight into today's world news. 61
Now you know why it really does matter what you believe. 63

Why It Matters What You Believe!

A note to my grandchildren and great grandchildren........... 65
ACKNOWLEDGMENTS **67**

Forward

One day I was thinking about my future grandchildren and great grand children who probably would be living around the year 2050, contemplating what kind of world they would be living in. What would I want them to know? As I thought about it, I decided the one issue that is timeless is a discussion about the existence of a creator, and the creator's relevance to how we live our lives.

Having just turned 71, I've done and seen a few things. After spending my younger years on my family's Indiana farm and attending school in a rural environment, similar to that depicted in the movie "The Hoosiers," I left home and eventually earned a degree in Civil Engineering at Purdue University.

Following a few years working in applied research, and highway and building design and construction, I took the plunge into building a construction business of my own from scratch. Over the next 30 plus years, the construction company grew to an annual sales volume of more than 100 million dollars, and a payroll of more than 250 people.

Along the way, I was involved in the development and operation of office buildings, a hotel and conference center, a restaurant, and a residential facility for the elderly. I've been active in the public policy areas of healthcare reform, public education and workforce training. Twice, I've tested the political waters by making unsuccessful runs for the Vermont State Senate.

As is usually the case, some of these ventures were successful and some were not, but all of them were learning experiences. I learned the necessity of doing my homework. I also learned that a key aspect of business success is creating an emotionally compelling vision, testing that vision against the marketplace; and painting a picture of that vision so that others can see themselves in it, can believe in it, and want to be a part of bringing that vision to reality.

I've also come to appreciate the power of belief, not only for the creator of the vision, but also for those who buy into that vision.

I've come to realize we all have multiple visions for our future, our families, our careers, our vacations, and our retirement. These visions are spawned by the beliefs that rule us. They are at the core of why we do what we do.

With that in mind, let's begin a journey that will show us how belief in a creator can change our perception of the purpose of our existence.

INTRODUCTION:
There is a war going on.

There is a war going on. This war has been in progress for thousands of years. In this war, millions have been imprisoned, tortured, and killed. In some cases this war is fought with guns and bombs, in others it is fought with laws and education.

In today's world this war is being fought on several fronts. Among those are the shooting war with Muslim terrorists, the partial ban on religion in most Muslim countries, and the United States court system's ban on acknowledging a creator in our public school system.

The driving force behind this war is humanity's inability to agree on whether or not there is a creator. And the inability - of those who believe there is a creator - to agree on what the creator is like and what the creator's expectations are.

This inability to agree on the existence and other aspects of a creator has resulted in the variations in value systems that are the fuel that keeps this war going.

Given all this, most people would agree, at least on a societal level, it really does matter what you believe, as well as what the society you live in believes.

But does it really matter what we believe on a personal level - that level located between our ears where each of us lives? I believe it does matter and you deserve to know why.

That's the reason for this book.

- Otto Engelberth

PART I:

Our Mind's Logic Points Us to a Creator

Paradigm; everybody has one.

Before beginning the discussion of our personal beliefs you need to be aware of the fact that each one of us has a set of assumptions, concepts, values, and practices that constitute our way of viewing reality. This is sometimes referred to as "our paradigm."

Our paradigms are the "box" where we think and live. It is the filter through which we screen, categorize, or reject information we receive, and it forms the basis for our actions. It simplifies our lives by creating short cuts in our thinking process.

What you may not have thought about is that many of our beliefs are based on incomplete assumptions about the real world. Some of those incomplete assumptions are because we lack knowledge. It may be that we have not assimilated the known knowledge, or possibly the knowledge we lack is not yet known. Today, knowledge is a fast changing commodity; it is estimated that the world's accumulated knowledge doubles every 24 months.

Also, some of our incomplete assumptions are the result of the fact that the real world is usually different from the way that we perceive things. This happens because our mind is selective in how it records the information it receives through our five senses. I experience this every time I look at the picture on my driver's license. I can't believe it is the same person that I see in the mirror every morning.

And finally, our beliefs are heavily influenced by the assumptions of the social groups that we are affiliated with. This happens because we tend to assimilate the beliefs of those we know and trust without examining the assumptions underlying those beliefs.

One assumption central to our paradigm is our concept of a creator. With that in mind, let's examine why the concept of a creator is so widely held.

Why most people believe there is a Creator.

So why would 90% of Americans as well as the vast majority of humanity, even the most remote peoples on earth, regardless of time in history, believe there is a creator? A major reason for man's belief in a creator is because his mind is pre-wired for logical thinking.

So what are logical arguments that support this almost universal belief in a creator?

The human dimension of time.

Albert Einstein, the great physicist, developed the theory of relativity. A key part of this theory is the concept that the fourth dimension is time. Like length, width, and height, time is a dimension that is an important part of our everyday lives.

We human beings think in the dimension of time. We are all familiar with the concept that events happen in a time sequence. We naturally think that every sequence of events has a beginning and an ending. So we naturally are inclined to think in terms of the universe having a beginning.

The law of "cause and effect" begs for an answer.

The law of cause and effect says that everything that exists is the result of some cause. For instance, parents cause a child's existence, the sun's heat warms the earth, gravity holds the planets in place, etc. So, it is natural for us to think that everything in the universe was caused by something.

However, if we follow that line of reasoning, something had to be the original cause of everything. We call the original cause the creator because the original effect had no normal cause.

Our human curiosity asks what drives the order and complexity of the universe.

We humans, by nature, are curious. This curiosity is on display from early childhood on. It drives us to explore and ask why things are the way they are. Over time, this curiosity has driven us to develop a vast storehouse of knowledge about everything that we are aware of.

As we learn more we are struck by the complexity and order of things, the vastness of the universe, the laws of physics, and the complexities of biology. Our logical response is that there is a grand design and that design originated with the creator.

Our human need to have a context for our existence.

We now know that our blueprint is contained in our DNA that comes into existence at our conception. Just as DNA contains the blueprint for our physical bodies, it also has the design for our mind and its core thinking processes. And it is in the make-up of these thinking processes that the framework for our concept of the creator being a spirit that relates to us exists.

Our concept of a spirit is derived from our concept of self. Our concept of self resides in our mind and we have a perception of its existence being separate from our bodies. This sense of self is prewired to believe that it has an eternal existence.

Our thinking processes are divided into two primary categories: our conscious mind and our subconscious mind. Our conscious mind does only a small part of our thinking because its function is to primarily be a real-time intermediary between our subconscious mind and the outside world.

On the other hand, our subconscious mind is the real workhorse. It regulates most of the functions of our bodies, stores all of our accumulated knowledge and all of our history. In addition, it operates all of our emotions and our senses. And finally, it is the place where almost all of our quality problem solving occurs.

Another key aspect of the subconscious mind is that it is prewired with a sense of right and wrong. This sense of right and wrong is what we refer to as our conscience. In most of us, this conscience considers wrong to be unfinished business (guilt) that needs to be dealt with.

Our minds perceive wrong to be a hindrance to our relationship with others, so it naturally assumes that wrong hinders our relationship with the creator.

Unanswered questions.

At this point we cannot prove the existence of a creator by the scientific method because it is only useful when dealing

Why It Matters What You Believe!

with measurable, material things. So we are left with trying to explain our universe in the absence of a creator.

Questions like:
- How did it all begin?
- How do we explain how the order and design of the universe came about?
- How did life come about?
- Why does the human mind's logic support the argument that there is a creator?

These are questions that challenge most thinking people.

Why? Because how we answer these questions has far reaching implications for us. Our thoughts, actions, how we live our lives and how we spend eternity could be impacted by our answer.

If you assume creation happened by chance, you have to ask, what are the odds against that happening?

Related Information

Most of us were taught that Darwin's theory of evolution is proven science. It turns out that this is just not so. There is no scientifically credible fossil evidence that supports his theory. And further, given what we now know about biology - more specifically cell structure and DNA - it is impossible for new species to evolve as Darwin envisioned.

If you want to examine this subject further, I suggest that you read Grant R. Jeffrey's book titled "CREATION: Remarkable Evidence of God's Design."

If our answer is that there is no creator, then it follows that we humans are the supreme beings on the earth and possibly the universe. We are in control. We make the rules. We are alone! Our existence begins at conception and ends at death.

However, if we believe that there is a creator and that we are a part of its creation, we are inclined to want to know what implications that has for us.

PART II

The Bible's Description of the Creator

What do we know about the Creator?

That depends on who you ask. Throughout recorded history people have been speculating about the existence of a creator, and if there is a creator, what the creator is like and what the creator's expectations are.

The ancient Egyptians had their sun gods. The Greeks had a variety of gods that served various purposes. At other times people would set up man-made idols as sort of "rabbit's foot" type gods. And the Romans even declared that their leader, the Caesar, was their god.

Of course, just because they called them god didn't mean that they were the creator of all that is in the universe. It would be a stretch to believe that a person or an image made of wood, metal or stone would be capable of doing that.

The words god and creator are not interchangeable. They don't necessarily mean the same thing. God is a title a person uses to describe an entity or object that they choose to worship or deify or idolize, while the word creator refers to the entity doing the creating.

For example, in the Christian Bible the Creator's name is Yahweh or Jehovah. The Creator is also called God because it is a title that reflects their view of the creator.

It turns out that one of the most detailed descriptions of the Creator is found in the Christian Bible. The Bible's authors wrote what they claimed the Creator told them to write. Over time, its validity has been confirmed by archeology, historical validation, prophecy's of future events that came to pass, and the fact that people's lives are changed by accepting and acting on the truths contained in it.

The Creator, from the Bible's perspective.

The Bible was written over a period of more than two thousand years.

It is made up of two parts, the Old Testament and the New Testament. (Note that the meaning of the word "testament" is similar to words "covenant" and "agreement").

The "Old Testament" is primarily a history of the nation of Israel and its covenant relationship with the Creator. It covers the time from the creation until approximately the year 400 BC. It was written by more than 30 different authors over a period of 1,500 years. Its authors include a shepherd, the nation's leaders, its historians, and its prophets.

The "New Testament" describes the new covenant between the Creator and man that was made possible by the Creator becoming a man in the person of Jesus Christ. It tells about Jesus' birth, life, death and resurrection, and explains what it all means for us individually.

All of its eight authors were contemporaries of Jesus. Of these, three - Matthew, a tax collector; and John and Peter, fishermen - were Jesus' disciples who spent three years of their adult lives with Him and personally saw most of the events that they wrote about. Luke was a Greek gentile convert and a trained physician. Two others, James and Jude were Jesus' younger half brothers. And Mark had traveled extensively with Peter and Paul. And finally, one of the more prolific New Testament writers, Paul, was one of the rising stars of the Jewish religious group called the Pharisees before his dramatic conversion to believing in Jesus as the promised messiah. Many speculate that he was in line to become the next great Jewish theologian because he trained under Gamaliel, who had been trained by Hillel, who is well known and respected even today.

All of these eight authors were committed to the truth of their message to the point where they were willing to suffer great persecution and even death because of it.

The two testaments are together because the New Testament is a fulfillment of over 200 prophecies in the Old Testament. The central theme of the Bible is about the Creator and His relationship with mankind.

Characteristics of the Creator.

The Bible describes the Creator as being a spirit who existed before anything else existed and who always will exist. The Creator is all-powerful, knows everything - past, present, and future - but has the capacity of viewing events in real time.

The Creator is holy. This means that the Creator is not a part of his creation but is set apart from it. Therefore, worshiping creation is not worshiping the Creator.

The Creator knows who He is. It's His creation; therefore, he demands our respect. And since the Creator's character is unchanging, ultimately, He will not allow His creation to continue forever in violation of His character. With that being said, we can take comfort in the knowledge that the Creator is just in all of His decisions.

The Creator has a different perspective than all of His created beings. The Bible states that the Creator's thoughts are not like our thoughts.

The Creator is involved and has a dynamic, real time relationship with all of His creation. That being said, He has already "seen the movie" of the past, present, and future, so He knows how it all turns out. It follows that the Creator knew you and me before creation.

The Creator is love in His being and actions. And because He is love, He did not create in order to control but for the purpose of having a relationship and to fulfill His purpose on earth. The Creator gives His created beings a free will, meaning that they have the right to choose whether or not to have a relationship with Him within the framework of His character.

The Bible says the Creator is also a multifaceted spirit. One aspect of His spirit that operates throughout His creation is referred to as the Holy Spirit. Another aspect of the Creator's spirit became a man, Jesus, His only Son.

No one (with the exception of Jesus) has seen the Creator because He is a spirit. He is located in a place that is called Heaven.

PART III

The Bible's Description of the Creation Process

Angels.

The Bible says that there are created entities that we normally can't see or directly detect except by the effect of their influence on our thinking process and what goes on around us.

One type of spirit-being the Creator created, before He created man, is the angel. There is a parallel between the angels and man in that it appears that the Creator's primary goal in creating them was fellowship. Individual angels have their own unique character and personality.

A particularly gifted and beautiful angel named Lucifer (also referred to as Satan and Devil) led a rebellion of one-third of the angels against the Creator and those angels that continue to serve Him. The rebellion failed and Satan and his followers, now referred to as demons, lost their positions in the service of the Creator in Heaven. This conflict has not been finally resolved and continues to this day.

Note that this is important for us to know because Satan is presently the primary spiritual influence on our earth and is the cause of human death and all of the evil that we experience and observe. The Bible also indicates that the devil is deceitful and lies.

Angels, being spirits, can't die or be destroyed. Furthermore, there is no indication that any of the angels who rebelled against the Creator have been, or will be, reconciled to Him.

The Old Testament account of physical creation.

The Old Testament book called Genesis is the first of five books of the Bible that are commonly referred to as "The Books of Moses."

Moses, their author, was an Israelite who was raised as a prince in the Egyptian Pharaoh's court and later was Israel's leader during the time of their exodus from Egypt about 1,440 to 1,400 BC. It was during this time that the books are believed to have been written.

We now know from our study of geology and anthropology, that the universe has a very, very long history, perhaps billions of years. So it is not surprising that the first chapter of the first book, called Genesis, gives a very condensed version of creation.

The Genesis account begins with the earth being a "shapeless chaotic mass with the Spirit of the Creator brooding over the dark vapors." Then creation occurred in seven successive periods of time.

1. Light and darkness were created.
2. The atmosphere was created.
3. The water levels receded, exposing the land masses; plant life flourished and reproduced itself.
4. The solar system planets and moon became visible on earth so that days, nights, and seasons could be identified.
5. The water teemed with fish and other life, and the skies were filled with birds of every kind.
6. The earth brought forth every kind of animal and reptile, and during this period of time the Creator created man, a male named Adam, and female named Eve, with a physical body having a spirit and character like Him. The Creator instructed man to multiply, fill the earth and

rule over the earth and all living beings, (Think of man's role as being the Kingdom of Heaven's "colonists" on earth).
7. The Creator was pleased with all that He had done so He stopped creating and rested. This is the period of time we are in now.

Related Information

The Bible describes the Creator's organizational structure as a Kingdom. So it will be helpful to know about the Creator's Kingdom and how it differs from a democracy.

For instance, in a democracy, property ownership resides with the citizen; in the Creator's Kingdom all property in His domain is owned by the King. Another title for the King in this ownership role is Lord. The King can give the right to use His property to anyone He chooses.

While democracies expand their domain by establishing democracies outside of their borders, Kings expand their domain by establishing colonies outside their domain.

While newly established democracies create their own laws and citizenship requirements, the citizens of colonies become citizens of the Kingdom and operate by the Kingdom's laws.

Democracies' leaders are voted into power by the will of the citizens, the Creator is the King because He created everything and therefore can't be voted out.

In a democracy, the leader must consult with legislature and high court; in the Creator's Kingdom, He has absolute authority.

His word is law. In a democracy, laws can be amended, revised, or revoked; in the Creator's Kingdom, His word is law and can't be changed.

In a democracy, the citizens choose their leader; in the Creator's Kingdom, He chooses the citizens. Since the Creator's

> *authority is absolute, He determines the standards of citizenship in His Kingdom.*
>
> *In a democracy the government is in a geographic location; in the Creator's Kingdom the authority is wherever He is. Also, since a King's name is the essence of His authority, the Creator can delegate that authority to anyone He pleases to act on His behalf by using His name.*

The Garden of Eden.

At the time that the Creator created Adam, He made him from dirt and breathed life in him in a place called the Garden of Eden. Originally, Adam and Eve were innocent because they had not experienced evil; therefore, they had no guilt. They communed with the Creator on a daily basis, fulfilled His purpose of dominion over the Garden, and lived in harmony with His Kingdom in Heaven.

As He did with the angels, The Creator gave man the option of rebelling against Him. He did this by planting the "tree of the knowledge of good and evil" in the Garden and told Adam and Eve not to eat its fruit because if they ate of it and experienced evil, they would eventually die.

Satan spoke to Eve and convinced her of the lie that she would not only not die, but if they ate the fruit, they would be like the Creator. So Eve ate the tree's fruit and convinced Adam to also eat it. Because of this act of rebellion they were doomed to die. They were doomed to die because Satan views man as the Creator's creation, he wants to use them in his struggle with the Creator and wants to ultimately destroy them.

Furthermore, Adam, Eve and succeeding generations now understood good and evil. With this act of rebellion against the Creator, Adam and Eve first experienced guilt. They realized that they were naked and tried to hide from the Creator. The

Creator then, in effect, started the first animal sacrifice by killing an animal to make clothes for Adam and Eve to wear as a covering for their shame.

Because of their rebellion, Adam and Eve lost their domain on earth as representatives of the Kingdom of Heaven and were banished from the Garden. The Creator did this because He also had planted "the tree of life" in the Garden and this tree's fruit, if eaten, would give them life forever in rebellion against the Creator, like the demons have.

The Creator's response to man's rebellion was brought about because fallen man's character is in conflict with His character. It can also be explained by how the Creator views mankind; He sees them as spirits. This is because He said "Let us make man like us, and the Creator is Spirit.

As in the case of the angels who are spirit beings, mankind's spirit never dies. However, in man's case, the Creator wanted to give mankind an opportunity to be reconciled to Him while they are alive in their earthly body.

The Creator's plan for reconciling man to Himself and reestablishing man's Creator-given earthly domain.

The Creator knew from the beginning that man would rebel against him because man was living on a planet where Satan is the primary spiritual influence. Furthermore, he knew that in this environment, man was incapable of doing anything to earn a relationship with the Creator because, by definition, in rebellion, man had become a Satan-led, self-centered being rather than a Creator-centered being.

So, before creation, the Creator developed a plan that would give man an opportunity to be forgiven for his rebellion, to be reconciled to his Creator, conquer death, and at the same time, reestablish the Kingdom of Heaven on earth. In addition, the Creator's plan would also, once and for all, conquer Satan and his demons, and set in motion a plan for taking them out of circulation by eventually confining them forever in a place called Hell.

The Creator's plan for doing this revolves around His decision to personally become a man and experience what it is like to be man in a world dominated spiritually by Satan and his demons.

About 2,000 years ago, the Creator accomplished this by becoming the biological father of a child conceived by a young Jewish virgin named Mary. She gave birth to a baby boy whom she named Jesus (we celebrate this event at Christmas time).

While in a human body, Jesus would experience Satan's temptations but would not give in to them. The Bible says that Jesus was without sin. This is important because it was the Creator's plan from the beginning that Jesus would pay the penalty for man's rebellion by dying in their place.

Jesus would prove to mankind that He was the Creator's Son by performing many supernatural miracles observed by thousands of people. Included in Jesus' miracles were the healing of hundreds of people's sicknesses and mental illnesses; and restoration of their limbs, eyesight, hearing, and ability to talk.

On two occasions Jesus fed thousands of people by expanding one person's meal in such a way that they were all fed with several meals left over. On another occasion He walked on water, on another He turned water into wine, and on another He calmed a violent storm by His verbal command.

Jesus even brought dead people back to life. His most dramatic raising of a dead person occurred just a few weeks before His own death and resurrection. This occurred when

Why It Matters What You Believe!

Jesus raised His good friend Lazarus even though he had died and his body was decomposing because it had been in a tomb for four days.

Eventually, the Creator would allow man, under Satan's influence, to whip and beat Jesus and then kill Him by crucifying Him. However, on the third day after Jesus died and was buried in a tomb guarded by soldiers, Jesus rose from the dead. After this He was seen by more than 500 people. And finally, His disciples observed Him ascend into Heaven 40 days later.

PART IV

The Creator Wants Us to Believe Him

What does the Creator ask of man?

So now that the Creator has paid the price for man's rebellion, what's left for man to do? Rather than tell you in my words, I'll let Jesus himself give you the answer by relating His conversation with a man who had that same question. This is recorded in John's Gospel. (Note that Jesus refers to the Creator as God because He, being the Creator of everything in the universe, is worthy of our praise and worship. So from this point forward I will refer to the Creator using the term "God.")

Gospel of John Chapter 3: Verses 1 thru 22 from the Living Bible

The following is quoted from the Living Bible with the exception of the author's notes in parentheses and the added italics in the text:

After dark one night a Jewish religious leader named Nicodemus, a member of the sect of the Pharisees, came for an interview with Jesus. "Sir," he said, "we all know that God has sent you to teach us. Your miracles are proof enough of this."
Jesus replied, "With all the earnestness I possess I tell you this: Unless you are born again, you can never get into the Kingdom of God."

"Born again!" exclaimed Nicodemus. "What do you mean? How can an old man go back into his mother's womb and be born again?"

Jesus replied, "What I am telling you so earnestly is this: Unless one is born of water (physical birth) and the Spirit, he cannot enter into the Kingdom of God. Man can only reproduce human life, but the Holy Spirit gives new life from heaven; so don't be surprised at my statement that you must be born again!

Just as you can hear the wind but can't tell where it comes from or where it will go next, so it is with the Spirit. We do not know on whom he will next bestow this life from heaven."

"What do you mean?" Nicodemus asked.

Jesus replied, "You, a respected Jewish teacher, and you don't understand these things? I am telling you what I know and have seen - and yet you won't believe me. But if you don't even believe me when I tell you about such things as these that happen among men, how can you possibly believe if I tell you what is going on in heaven? For only I, the Messiah (Son of Man), have come to earth and will return to heaven again.

And as Moses in the wilderness lifted up the bronze image of a serpent on a pole, even so I must be lifted up on a pole (cross), so that anyone who believes in me will have eternal life. *For God so loved the world that he gave his only Son so that anyone who believes in him shall not perish but have eternal life.*

God did not send his Son into the world to condemn it, but to save it.

There is no eternal doom awaiting those who trust him to save them. But those who don't trust him have already been tried and condemned for not believing in the only Son of

God. Their sentence is based on this fact; that the Light from heaven came into the world, but they loved the darkness more than the Light, for their deeds were evil.

They hated the heavenly Light because they wanted to sin in the darkness. They stayed away from the Light for fear their sins would be exposed and they would be punished. But those doing right came gladly to the light to let everyone see that they are doing what God wants them to.

With God it's always been about belief.

What Jesus is saying is that our "default" situation is one of eternal doom. If we want to have eternal life, we have to recognize our need for a savior, believe that Jesus is God's Son and accept what Jesus has done to reconcile us to God. When we do this, we are spiritually reborn by God's Holy Spirit and we gain the free gift of eternal life and citizenship in the Kingdom of God.

About now you may be thinking that this is all too simple. In fact, you may be confused because you are under the impression that you earn eternal life through the "points system," by being good, living by the rules, giving money, helping other people, or going through some ritual or maybe even by whom you are related to, or some group you are associated with. You may even think that you will need the approval of a human or organizational "gate keeper" who controls your access to God and Heaven.

Contrary to what many people think, with God it's always been about belief.

When listing the ancestry of Abraham in the book of Genesis, its writer, Moses, highlights the fact that God's presence resided with those who believed God.

However, because of Satan's influence, not many people chose to believe God. By the time Noah came along, some 1,500 years after the creation of Adam, he was the only one of all the people on earth at that time who believed and walked with God.

God was so grieved with man's almost total disregard for their Creator that He decided to destroy all of them except Noah and his family in a great flood. They avoided drowning because Noah believed God's weather forecast for 125 years in the future and built the ark as God had instructed.

After the flood, God decided on a different approach to sustaining His presence with man on an earth whose primary spiritual influence is God's adversary, Satan. That new approach was to set aside a nation of people with whom God would make His presence known. And further, that nation would become the stage on which God would become a man, pay the price for man's rebellion against God, eventually subdue Satan and his demons, and set up God's Kingdom on earth.

Abraham believed God.

About 350 years after the flood, God chose a man, named Abraham, to be the person whose descendants would become the nation with whom God's spirit would reside. The Bible says that Abraham was chosen by God because Abraham believed God.

For the first four generations, Abraham's family functioned like a nomadic clan in the region we know as Israel. Note that Abraham's grandson was originally named Jacob, but was renamed "Israel," and that became the name of the nation.

Because of a severe drought, Jacob and his twelve sons and families - about 70 people in all - migrated to the Nile delta in

Egypt as guests of the Egyptian king. About 430 years later, they had become slaves of the Egyptians, and their number had grown to more than 600,000 men plus women and children.

Moses believed God.

It was at this point that God determined that Israel was ready to become the nation with whom He would dwell. He recruited Moses to be the person that God would use to free the Israelites from Egyptian bondage, organize them into a nation, and lead them back to their promised land in what is now Israel.

God was able to use Moses because he believed God and was willing to do what God told him to do. Following God's instructions, Moses delivered God's ten plagues that convinced Egypt to let the Israelites leave Egypt.

After they left Egypt, Moses, following God's instruction, set up the nation's system of government, legal system, and laws and rules. These laws and rules were wide-ranging, covering property rights, taxation; public health and personal hygiene; the people's relationships with each other, and their relationship with God.

Their relationship with God centered in a movable structure referred to as a "tabernacle." It housed rooms and utensils for various animal, bird, and grain sacrifices that were offered as a substitute death to cover the people's guilt for the wrong they had done.

In one room, called the Holy of Holies, was a gold-covered box, referred to as "The Ark of the Covenant." The box's lid had two gold cherubim facing each other with wings outstretched. The top of the lid between the two cherubim was called the place of God's mercy where God's Spirit dwelled with the Israelites.

However, even with God's presence among them, most Israelites did not believe God.

Of the 600,000 men who left Egypt, only two actually entered into the present land of Israel because they were the only ones, besides Moses, who believed God's promise to enable them to conquer the land's inhabitants.

Think about it - these were the same people who saw the plagues that God brought on the Egyptians: the Nile river turned to blood, the plague of frogs, lice, flies, animals dying, boils, extreme hail, locusts, three days of darkness, and the death of the Egyptians' first born males.

They walked through the God-parted Red Sea on dry ground, then looked back and saw the Egyptian army, who were following them, drown as the water closed in on them.

They ate the manna and quail, and drank the water that God provided them. They saw the cloud by day and the nightly pillar of fire that God used to guide them in the wilderness. They felt the earth shake and heard God speak to Moses at Mount Sinai. They experienced God's power in enabling them to crush the army of Amalek.

And yet they chose not to believe God.

In fact, over the next 900 plus years that are described in the Old Testament, many generations of Israelites chose not to believe God. Most often they found it more appealing to worship man-made images called idols. Eventually, the Ark of the Covenant was lost. They were conquered by neighboring nations, most were taken captive, and they were no longer an independent nation until 1948 - approximately 2,500 years later.

PART V

Why is it so Difficult for Man to Believe God?

We want to hang on to the illusion that we are in control.

Back in the 1950s, the singer Frank Sinatra sang the song titled "My Way," written by Paul Anka, Jacques Revaux, Gilles Thibaut, and Claude Francois. The words of this song are those of a person who has lived his life believing that he is in control.

And now, the end is here
And so I face the final curtain
My friend, I'll say it clear
I'll state my case, of which I'm certain
I've lived a life that's full
I traveled each and ev'ry highway
And more, much more than this, I did it my way

Regrets, I've had a few
But then again, too few to mention
I did what I had to do and without exception
I planned each charted course, each careful step along
The byway
And more, much more than this, I did it my way

Yes, there were times, I'm sure you knew
When I bit off more than I could chew
But through it all, when there was doubt

I ate it up and spit it out
I faced it all and I stood tall and did it my way

I've loved, I've laughed and cried
I've had my fill, my share of losing
And now, as tears subside, I find it all so amusing
To think I did all that
And may I say, not a shy way,
Oh, no, oh, no, not me, I did it my way

For what is a man, what has he got?
If not himself, then he has naught
To say the things he truly feels and not the words of
One who kneels
The record shows I took my blows and did it my way!
Yes, it was my way

    Most of us can relate to the words of this song. Especially when things are going well, it's easy to think we are in control. But believing we are in control is an illusion because we really don't control much. We don't control the circumstances of our birth, who our parents are, where we are born, the color of our eyes and skin, our time in history, the genetic aspects of our mental and physical health, and much of our environment, including the behavior of other people.

    However, our desire to be in control stands in the way of believing God, because believing God leads to the recognition that God is in control. Many of us try to get around giving up control by adopting one of the counterfeits of belief.

Belief and its counterfeits.

By definition "to believe" is a verb that indicates a person's confidence in the truth or existence of something not immediately susceptible to rigorous proof. And "faith" is the noun that describes what a person believes.

Implied in this definition is the concept that the person doing the believing will act on the basis of their belief. So, if a person believes there is a Creator, and the Creator has a purpose for creating them, that person would do what the Creator wants them to do.

Of course, there is always the option to not believe. An extreme example would be those that make the assumption that the Creator does not exist.

Another option is to "hedge your bet" by adopting one of the "counterfeits" for believing the Creator (God). Some adopt *hope* instead of belief. An example of hope would be a person who says, "I'm a pretty good person; if there is a God, I hope He lets me into Heaven." The person who hopes says, "I will get it sometime, my way," vs. the believing person who says, "I have it now, and I will act on what I believe."

Another counterfeit for belief is the knowledge that comes from our five senses, sight, smell, hearing, touch, and taste. The person that adapts the *sense knowledge* alternative demands proof. They will say things like, "When I see it or feel it then I will believe it." They also might say, "seeing is believing," when in reality, many times, "believing is seeing."

And finally, *mental assent* is another belief counterfeit. The person who says that they believe the Bible to be the true Word of God but fails to act on it is a mental assenter. The mental assenter, in effect, says "The Bible is true but not in my case."

In the next sections, we'll see that choosing to believe the Creator is not a simple process.

Belief is difficult for us because of how our mind works.

For the purposes of this next discussion, I've included a diagram that shows some of the aspects of how our minds work; see page 32.

The box representing the conscious mind is small relative to the circle representing the subconscious mind because its function is very limited. It is geared toward short term real-time thinking and tends to be logic-oriented.

On the other hand, our subconscious mind is one of the real wonders of the universe. It monitors and interprets inputs from our five senses: sight, hearing, touch, smell, and taste. It controls and directs all of our body's systems, stores all of our memories, formulates our communications and actions, and works on problems that it deems important, 24 hours per day 7 days per week.

Our subconscious mind tends to be driven more by emotion and feelings.

It contains the entities and characteristics that are described by the terms: self, spirit, heart, soul, gut, passion, and paradigm.

Experts tell us that we think between 15,000 and 60,000 thoughts per day. That works out to a range of 20 to 80 thoughts per minute! Much of this happens in our subconscious minds without our being aware of it.

However, when we dream we become aware of typical random thoughts generated by this process. These random thoughts also pop up when we try to concentrate or focus our thinking. Perhaps you have experienced these distractions when listening to a lecture, shooting a basketball foul shot, or hitting a golf tee shot.

Occasionally we give direction to our subconscious mind. We do this by requesting information or a solution to a problem.

But contrary to what you may believe, *we really don't directly control our subconscious mind.* Most of the time it just churns away thinking 20 to 80 thoughts per minute!

The best we can do is to exert influence in two ways. First, we can do this by controlling the information and experiences that make up the data bank our mind uses to create our thoughts. And secondly, we influence the subconscious mind's thought process by establishing a purpose-driven goal or vision that our subconscious mind agrees with.

For example, we experience how this works when we make a new year's resolution. With our logic-driven conscious mind we make a resolution to lose weight this year. Then we wonder why we are not able to make good on that resolution. The reason for our failure is that we have not made an emotionally compelling case to get the buy-in of our emotionally driven subconscious minds.

To further complicate things, the Bible says that we also have outside spiritual influences on our subconscious thinking processes. These spiritual influences include Satan and his demons who are evil influences, and God's Holy Spirit who is an influence for good.

Notice that I've shown these spiritual influences in solid line boxes that are outside the subconscious mind. The dotted line spiritual boxes in the subconscious mind represent the situation where a person allows a spirit to take up residence in their mind.

The Bible describes the situation where Satan and his demons take residence in a person's mind as "demon possession." These people exhibit behavior which we would characterize as being evil. You may have noticed that this seems to be a popular subject of many Hollywood movies.

The dotted line for the Holy Spirit represents situations where we choose to believe Jesus, accept His free gift of eternal life, and invite the Holy Spirit to dwell in us.

As an aside, you will also note that these two boxes have different definitions of truth. The Holy Spirit represents *absolute truth*, the Devil is called *the deceiver and a liar*, and our subconscious mind's paradigm could be called *relative truth*. Keep in mind that belief doesn't create truth and unbelief doesn't destroy truth.

So what does all this have to do with believing God?

The Bible says that man believes God with the heart. It is clear that it is not referring to our organ that pumps blood, but is referring to an aspect of our subconscious mental process. Since we have made the case that we don't have direct control over this process, how do we come to believe God?

Related Information

You will find this description of how our mind works to be useful in your roles as a leader and communicator. If we are to be effective in leadership and communication it is important to remember that we need to get the buy-in of the subconscious minds of those that we are leading or communicating with.

Think of this process as bypassing their conscious minds and communicating directly with their subconscious minds, that part that they don't directly control! In order to succeed, your communication must be emotionally driven and resonate with each person's purpose and values that reside in their subconscious minds.

Needless to say, successful communicators and leaders do their homework. They know the values and underlying purposes of those they are dealing with! As you might expect, your task will be easier if the group that you are dealing with have similar values and life purposes.

Figure 1: Otto's Diagram of the Mind and Its Functions

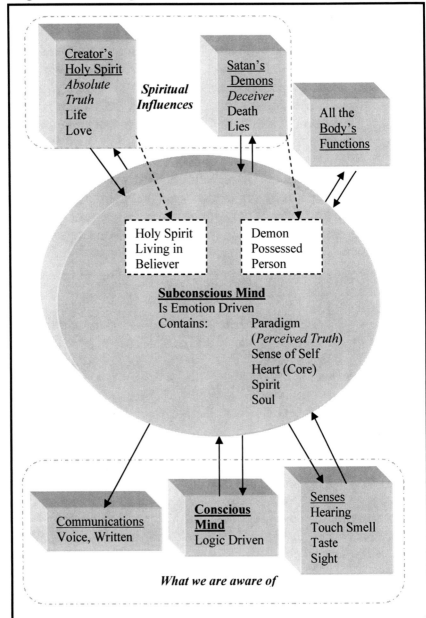

The role that emotions play in our believing God.

Every day we make decisions that are emotionally driven. Marketers know this. That's why they are able to convince us to buy beverages by associating them with good times or get us to buy a car by appealing to our pride.

In fact, there are a lot of different emotions that come into play in our decision making process. Some of them are positive and some are negative.

Those that fall into the positive category are love, joy, peace, forgiveness, friendship, freedom, generosity, hope, light, order, and thankfulness.

Examples of negative emotions are hatred, greed, sadness, despair, fear, guilt, worry, anger, bondage, darkness, loneliness, chaos, and doubt.

The thing to keep in mind is that our decisions that are made as the result of positive emotions are much more sustainable than those that are the result of negative emotions. A way to think of this principle is that we are drawn by the pleasure that we experience from positive emotions.

In contrast, a decision made as a result of a negative emotion usually results in us doing the minimum action necessary to avoid the pain caused by those negative emotions.

In Jesus' conversation with Nicodemus He said, "For God so loved the world that He gave His only Son so that anyone who believes in Him will have eternal life."

Jesus also said that we should love the Lord our God with all of our hearts, with all of our minds, and all of our souls. And further, we should love our neighbors as we love ourselves.

At the time of Jesus' birth, angels appeared to the shepherds saying, "I bring you good news of great joy for all people ----

Glory to God in the highest, peace on earth and goodwill to man---."

You will notice that God is using the words love, joy, peace and goodwill to describe His feelings toward mankind and the emotional impact His presence will have on them.

While each of us approaches the decision to believe God from the perspective of our own life's experiences, the following are some of the emotionally compelling reasons many people give for making that choice:

- They are drawn to have a relationship with the Creator of the universe who loves them and knows them by name.
- They want freedom from the guilt for the wrong that they have done.
- They want to have freedom from the bondage that they have to their destructive habits and addictions.
- They want the hope of eternal life rather than the fear of eternal damnation.
- They want a loving relationship with their Creator and fellow believers rather than a life of loneliness, hatred, greed, sadness, and despair.
- They want a life that has eternal significance rather than a life of temporal uncertainty and chaos.

God's Holy Spirit enables man to believe in Him.

The Bible says that our decision to believe God happens because God's Holy Spirit reveals these truths to us.

Earlier, we discussed how God's original approach was to have his presence be with individuals who believed Him. We noted that that approach was a disappointment because 1,500 years after Adam's creation, Noah was the only person who believed God.

Later, God chose a nation that he would dwell with. As we also discussed, that approach, over time, also became a disappointment.

Next, God dwelled on earth in the person of His Son, Jesus. While some believed in Him, most people did not, as evidenced by the fact that they supported Jesus' execution by crucifixion.

In conversations with His disciples, Jesus told them that after he returned to Heaven, they were to wait in Jerusalem until He would send the Holy Spirit to be with them. This happened, 10 days after Jesus ascended into Heaven, while the disciples were praying together on the Jewish Festival Day of Pentecost.

To them, and the people in their vicinity, the Holy Spirit's impact was unmistakable. They heard a rushing wind from Heaven, and saw small flames of fire above their heads. The Spirit gave them the ability to speak the languages of the people visiting for the Festival day, and gave them boldness and understanding to preach the gospel of Jesus and the power to heal people's sicknesses.

The spiritual rebirth that Jesus' disciples experienced at Pentecost literally changed the world. About 3,000 people became believers in Christ that day. And within 300 years, Christianity would become the official faith of the Roman Empire.

Clearly, the Holy Spirit was a key influence on those new believers' decisions to believe Jesus and accept His gift of eternal life. Why is this? The Bible says that it is impossible for us to believe God unless the Holy Spirit reveals Him and draws us to Him.

In the third chapter of God's Revelation to John, God uses a word picture to describe how this works. He said, "Here I am! I stand at the door and knock. If anyone hears my voice and opens the door, I will come in and eat with him, and he with me."

PART VI

Being Spiritually Reborn into God's Family

What happens when we are spiritually born again?

One way to describe being spiritually born again, in contemporary terms, would be to say that the believing person discards their old paradigm and adopts the paradigm of the Kingdom of God. However, it is much more than that; the Bible says that "the Believer becomes a new creature in Christ."

What did He mean when Jesus told Nicodemus that he needed to be "born again" if he wanted to see the Kingdom of God?

You may recall that, earlier in this book, we discussed how Adam and Eve rebelled against God by eating the "forbidden fruit of the knowledge of good and evil tree." You may also recall how this resulted in them, and future generations, losing the intimate relationship with God they had enjoyed in the Garden of Eden.

From God's perspective, rebellious mankind is spiritually incompatible with Him. So in order to reestablish God's intimate relationship with mankind, God needed to provide a way to fix man's spirit. Jesus called the process of fixing man's spirit, "being spiritually born again."

By using the word "born" to describe this process, Jesus is implying that our reborn spirit is made new and will continue to mature over time.

To get a picture of how this works, think of Jesus' conception, birth, and growing up to become a mature person. Jesus' spirit was compatible with God the Father's spirit because He was conceived by the joining together of the Holy Spirit with His mother Mary. In a similar way, our spirit becomes compatible with God the Father when our spirit is joined together with the Holy Spirit when we invite Him to dwell in us. That is why we are called "new creatures in Christ."

God's relationship with us.

When reading the New Testament's Gospels, we notice that Jesus makes a lot of references to God's Kingdom. We soon realize that our spiritually reborn life is not about religion but a relationship. It's about living life on a different plane within God's Kingdom.

We get to know the King; He is awesome! He has been and will be around forever. He goes by a different clock; His day is like one thousand of our years. He made everything and owns everything, and that includes us. That's why we call Him Lord.

It turns out that the King has known us for a very long time, even before He created the earth. We find that He knows all about us, but He chooses not to remember all the things for which we have asked Him to forgive us. In fact, the Bible says that the King forgets because His Son Jesus paid the penalty for our rebellion. So when the King sees us, He views us as perfect persons, because He sees Jesus' perfection and not our imperfection.

The King tells us that we are His friend, and He has loved us even when we were in rebellion against Him. That is why His Son, Jesus, went to the cross.

We find that we have duel-citizenship - citizens of the country of our physical birth and naturalized citizens of the kingdom of our new spiritual birth, the Kingdom of God. Our name is written down in Heaven's registry.

In addition to our Kingdom citizenship, we have all of the privileges that come with being a member of the King's family because we are His adopted sons and daughters. We are siblings of all of the other people who have accepted God's free gift of eternal life as well as Jesus Christ himself.

Jesus' central role in the Kingdom.

As you might expect, Jesus is involved in the Kingdom in a big way. First of all, He was one with God from the beginning, and; therefore, was the Creator and ruler of the Kingdom of Heaven. He became a human being, died on a cross, conquered death, and was raised from the dead for the ultimate purpose of reestablishing man's role of dominion on earth; the role that Adam and Eve abandoned when they rebelled against God. That's why Jesus is referred to as "the second Adam."

So, where is Jesus now and what is He doing? The Bible says that He is in the Royal Court of the Kingdom of Heaven, sitting on the right hand of God, and is our advocate to the King's Court.

However, His role does not end there. At some future date (we'll talk more about when, later) Jesus will meet us in the air and take us to Heaven. The Bible says that the believers who have died will rise first and then the believers who are alive will meet Him in the air.

When this happens, all of us will have new bodies that are like the new body Jesus had after His resurrection from the dead. These new bodies will be similar to those that we have now in that our appearance will be recognizable, we will be able to think, talk, eat, and be touched. However, these new bodies are different in that they will not be constrained by space.

All of this will take place in "a twinkling of an eye" and not be visible to those remaining on earth. Their only clue that something has happened is that all of the believers will have vanished.

After we are gone, life on earth will deteriorate. Satan will have his way and evil will prevail. During this time, more than half of the world's population will die from starvation, disease, war and natural disasters. The Bible says that if God would not have intervened, all of mankind would have been eliminated from earth. It will be a time that ends with, what the Bible refers to as, "the seven years of tribulation."

It is at the end of this tribulation that a Satan-controlled leader, referred to as the Antichrist, will gather the nations of the world together to carry out, what will turn out to be, the last military battle in a place in Israel, called the plains of Armageddon. It takes place in Israel because Satan knows that if he can destroy Israel, he will have eliminated the last reminder of God on earth.

It is the last battle because Jesus will very visibly return to earth with a host of angels and bring all of the believers with Him. He will crush the evil physical and spiritual forces that are running rampant on earth. Satan and his demons will be bound and cast into Hell and Jesus will set up His earthly kingdom in Jerusalem and rule over those people who have survived the tribulation for a period of 1,000 years.

The Bible says that the reason Jesus brings the believers with Him when He returns to earth is because they will rule with Him. The Bible says that the believers are "Priests of God and shall reign on earth."

During Jesus' 1,000 year reign there will be unparalleled peace and prosperity. You may have heard the phrase "beating swords into plow shares." this is the time when that happens. People will live for hundreds of years and there will be a population explosion.

After the 1,000 years, Satan will be released from hell for a short period of time to rally some of the descendents of the tribulation survivors who have chafed under Jesus' rule. They, following Satan's leadership, will attempt to rebel against Jesus' rule and they will be crushed. Satan and his demons will again be bound and cast into hell forever.

The consequences of unbelief.

About now you may be wondering what will happen to those who choose not to believe Jesus? You recall, from Jesus' conversation with Nicodemus, that man's "default position" is eternal doom. Well, the Bible says that this is the time when they also will be raised from the dead, bow their knee and acknowledge that Jesus is who He said He is. They will then be judged by Jesus and be cast into Hell forever. (It pains me to write this, but I have to because that's what the Bible says.)

PART VII

Successful "Kingdom Living"

God's priority.

With this glimpse of the future, how should believers prioritize their lives? For the nonbeliever their priority is survival. According to the renowned psychologist, Abraham Maslow, the priorities of most humans are in this order: air, water, food, clothes, housing, protection, security, preservation, self-actualization, and significance.

However, Jesus said that we are to make it our first priority to seek the Kingdom of God and align ourselves with God's priority. He promises us that when we do these two things, our needs will be met.

So, what is God's priority? Just before returning to Heaven, Jesus told his disciples that all authority has been given to Him in Heaven and on earth, and His priority is that they go throughout the world, preaching the "good news of salvation" to everyone everywhere.

In addition, they are to baptize those that accepted the "Good News," in the name of the Father (God), Son (Jesus), and the Holy Spirit. This act of baptism was to be an outward confirmation of their inward acceptance of who God is and what He has done for them.

And finally, the disciples were to teach those who believed the "Good News" how to live successful lives as members of God's Kingdom.

Words matter in God's Kingdom.

The Bible says that if you confess with your mouth, "Jesus is Lord," and believe in your heart that God raised Him from the dead, you will be saved. So a key to successful Kingdom living is that our words do matter.

Assuming that we have integrity, the words that we speak become an internal memory record and an outward confirmation of our thoughts and beliefs. Unfortunately, the words that we speak also become boundaries that constrain our actions.

As unbelievers, we were constrained when we spoke words such as: I can't, I'm not a good person, I don't have talent, I don't have ability, I haven't got strength, I don't have the resources, I am limited by my color or nationality or heritage, I don't have an education, I am too short or too tall, or I am not a good speaker. We said these words because they represent what we see when we see ourselves in the world's mirror. They also are an indication that we believe we are limited by what we could do in our own strength.

The Bible says that the same principles regarding words also apply to God. The Bible claims to be God's Word. Therefore, it reflects the thoughts and character of God. In fact, God's words are eternal because the Bible says that even if Heaven and earth were to pass away, His Word does not change.

This concept is illustrated further in John's Gospel when he begins by stating "In the beginning was the Word, and the Word was with God, and the Word was God." In this statement, John is calling Jesus "the Word" in order to make the point that He is God and that God is defined by God's words.

So why is this important? Well, when we confess that Jesus is Lord, we are recognizing that He owns us, and because He owns us over time we come to realize that our existence is defined and guided by God's words, not man's words.

The Bible (God's Word) says that we are new creatures in Christ and being new creatures:
- We are loved and accepted by God.
- We can do all things through Christ who strengthens us.
- We have God's strength.
- We have God's wisdom.
- We have God's ability.
- We have God dwelling in us.
- We have God's love in us.
- We have the capacity to love other people because God loves them.
- We have a vision for our eternal future.
- We have meaning and purpose for our lives.
- We have the promise that our actions have eternal significance.
- We have God's strength to resist Satan's temptations.
- We have peace because God has forgiven us for our sin and rebellion.
- We have motivation to take care of our bodies because that is where God dwells.

As you can see by this list, as we replace our words with God's words we have the tools for supernatural Kingdom living.

We need to learn God's word for our mental health.

Some of us want to skip this class and that's a big mistake. Why is this?

The reason we need to learn God's Word is for our mental health.

In an earlier section we discussed how our mind works and the fact that we really don't directly control our subconscious mind. And it follows that the best we can do is to control the information and experiences that make up the data bank that our mind uses to create our thoughts. It follows that the quality of our thoughts are greatly influenced by the quality of that stored information. And if you are like me, your mind has accumulated a lot of "garbage."

We also discussed the spiritual influences on our subconscious thinking processes. These spiritual influences include Satan and his demons who are evil influences and God's Holy Spirit who is an influence for good.

When we choose to believe Jesus, accept His free gift of eternal life, and invite the Holy Spirit to dwell in us, our mind becomes the prize in a spiritual battle between Satan and the Holy Spirit. We are not passive in this struggle. The information we've stored in our minds are weapons that are used in this battle. Needless to say, Satan uses our "garbage" to his advantage. It's only as we absorb truths of God's Word into our minds that we give the Holy Spirit the weapons that He needs to win this battle.

The Bible refers to this process as the "renewing of our minds." For most of us, this is an ongoing process that is one of the keys to our developing an intimate relationship with God.

Having a relationship with God.

The Bible says that God is a spirit. Think about it; how do we get to know a spirit? Not just any spirit, but one that created everything, is all powerful, knows everything, but also has the unique capability to function in real time like we do?

The Bible tells us a lot about God, but how do we really know Him and have a relationship with Him? We can't use our five senses (sight, hearing, taste, touch, and smell) as sources of information.

The answer can be found in our earlier discussion about how our mind works. Remember, I made the point that most of our thinking processes take place in our subconscious mind, beyond our awareness and direct control. I also showed how most of the Holy Spirit's influence happens directly with our subconscious mind without our being aware that it is happening.

Clearly, this relationship is not like any we have ever had before.

Fortunately, we have a model for what an ideal relationship between a person and God looks like. That model is the life of Jesus.

Jesus' relationship was ideal because, from childhood on the Holy Spirit was with Him, empowering Him to resist all temptation to sin, giving Him the insight to know and understand the meaning of what we call the Old Testament, and revealing to Jesus who He was and what His role would be in carrying out God's plan.

But how did Jesus nurture His relationship with God? He did it via the process called prayer. The Gospels indicate that Jesus spent as much as four hours each day praying alone. Jesus' prayer was a two way conversation; Jesus talking to God and God talking to Jesus.

To get some idea of Jesus' part of this conversation we need to examine the model prayer that Jesus gave to his disciples.

Our Father in Heaven,
Hallowed be your name,
Your Kingdom come,
Your will be done on earth as it is in Heaven.

Give us today our daily bread.
Forgive us our debts, as we forgive our debtors.
And lead us not into temptation, but deliver us from the evil.
For yours is the Kingdom and the power and the glory forever.
Amen

Jesus' prayer opens with worship and closes with praise. He reflects on who God is, where He is located, and shows respect for God's name because of all that it represents. His worship also reflects on the desirability of God's Heavenly Kingdom becoming operational on earth; and that Jesus is in agreement with what God wants done on earth.

Next, Jesus moves on to housekeeping items. He asks that His daily needs be met. Jesus then asks for a clean slate with the Father, with the full understanding that that is only possible if he has a clean slate with his fellow man. And finally, Jesus acknowledges that He needs power and direction from the Father in order to resist Satan's temptations.

While it is not clear which form of communication He received from God, it is clear that God did communicate with Him. This is reflected in Jesus' comments. He stated that He was only empowered to do the miracles that were assigned to Him by God and He only said the things that God instructed Him to say.

We almost get the sense that in these prayer sessions, God revealed to Jesus all of the things that were going to happen during the course of His day. Nothing was a surprise to Him. We get a glimpse of this process when Jesus was praying in the Garden of Gethsemane the night before His trial and His execution by crucifixion.

God revealed to Jesus what was going to happen. His disciple, Judas, would facilitate His capture by the religious guards. He would spend the night and the next morning being badgered and savagely beaten by the religious guards and the Roman soldiers. And in the afternoon the soldiers would nail His hands and feet to a cross and let Him hang there until He would die.

The Bible says that Jesus asked God if it was necessary for Him to be the one to do this. After all, this was the first time that God would allow Him to suffer physical harm. He was so stressed that He sweat real drops of blood. We are not told about God's side of the conversation, but finally Jesus agreed to do it.

Probably the thing that He struggled with the most was the knowledge that God would not intervene in the process because His dying on the cross was the ultimate purpose for His human existence. He was going to the cross bearing the burden of all of the sin of mankind. His death would be the substitute for the punishment that man deserved for rebelling against God. His death would make it possible for man to be spiritually reborn and have an intimate relationship with God.

So, what about those of us who are spiritually reborn - do we develop our intimate relationship with God the same way Jesus did? Yes and no. Yes, we nurture our relationship with God the same way Jesus did except that we are entering this relationship from a different starting point. Our starting point was a life in rebellion against God that we lived prior to being spiritually reborn. And because of that life, we bring a lot more mental clutter into our relationship with God than Jesus did.

Our clutter probably includes guilt, trauma, broken relationships, destructive pleasures, broken promises, personal failure, and the need to be in control. All of these are toxic to any relationship, but unlike our fellow humans, God knows all about us, loves us unconditionally, and the Holy Spirit shows us that we can put these things behind us, because of what Jesus did for us on the cross.

This is important because our relationship with God grows when we do things together with Him; in order for that to happen we need to be able to hear God's voice, believe what He says, and be willing to act on it.

Jesus lets us use His name.

Before going to the Garden of Gethsemane to pray, Jesus and His disciples had the Passover Supper together in a place referred to as the "upper room." During the meal He told His disciples that the next day He would be killed and after three days in the tomb, He would be brought back to life and then would return to Heaven. In Heaven, Jesus would resume his position with God and the Holy Spirit that He had before coming to earth as a human being.

Jesus then told them that they would be better off after He returned to Heaven. They would be better off because He would not only send the Holy Spirit to be with them, like He had been, but also the Holy Spirit would be in them individually. He also said the Holy Spirit, living in them, would dramatically change how they lived their lives.

While Jesus was with them, they were inclined to ask Him to do things for them. However, in the future, with the Holy Spirit living in them, they could directly ask God to do things for them on the authority of Jesus' name. Jesus told them that the reason God would grant the requests that they made in Jesus' name was to bring glory to God.

Do you remember our earlier discussion of how kingdoms work? We said that kings transfer their authority by allowing subjects to use the king's name. This is what Jesus is doing.

This is a big deal! Jesus is talking about the full range of requests; from those that we would consider as minor to those that we would consider to be miracles. He went on to say that they would even do miracles that were greater than those that He did while on the earth.

Our character and actions say a lot about our relationship with God.

That same night Jesus emphasized how important it would be for the disciples "to live in Him, and Him in them." To illustrate what He meant by this He used the word picture of a vineyard.

In this illustration, Jesus identified Himself as the vine, the believers as the branches tied to the vine, and the fruit being attached to the branches. And finally, it is God who tends the vineyard.

Since the purpose of the vineyard is to grow God's kind of fruit, this is the only fruit that the tender of the vineyard cares about; so he pays a lot of attention to the branches. Those that produce God's kind of fruit are pruned so that they produce more. Those branches that don't produce fruit are cut off and burned.

So what are these fruits that our lives will exhibit when we have a relationship with Jesus? The Bible lists them as follows:
- Love
- Joy
- Peace
- Patience
- Kindness
- Goodness
- Faithfulness

- Gentleness
- Self control

Love is at the top of the list because it is, literally, what makes the world go around. Love is the reason for creation. Love motivated God to create us. And after man rebelled against God, love motivated God to send His Son to be born as a man and to pay the price that was necessary for our reconciliation to Him.

To give us an idea of how important love is, the Bible says that anything that we might do for God will be of no eternal value unless it is done in love. And the only way we are able to exhibit God's love is to have Him live in us.

And finally, all of these kinds of fruit are a reflection of God's character.

Love helps us avoid the "School of Hard Knocks."

There is an old saying that says if we are not willing to learn what other people have already found out, we are destined to learn by "the school of hard knocks with the colors black and blue."

When we arrived as a newborn baby, we didn't come with a manual containing instructions on how to complete our mental and physical development, how to maintain our minds and bodies, and the warranty conditions that guarantee a successful life.

In our early years we are almost totally dependent on our parents to provide us with proper nourishment, care, and guidance. Included in the guidance part is informing us about things we shouldn't do. They informed us because they loved us and didn't want us to get hurt. In a way, they were teaching us that life is like a mine field that we all have to walk through, and they wanted to show us where the mines that they knew of were located.

Unfortunately, for most of us, we stop listening to our parents during our teenage years, so we stop learning where the mines are. In some cases, we start listening to our peers who tell us the mines that our parents told us about aren't in the minefield of life after all, and even if they are there, they won't hurt us. And besides, it is exciting to see how close we can get to the mines without stepping on them.

Over time, we come to realize that there is a price to be paid for stepping on life's land mines. They cost us our time, our resources, our relationships, our health, and sometimes even our life.

The Bible says that God loves us and only wants what's best for us. Being our Creator, He knows where all of the land mines of life are, and He wants to guide us through our mine field. To do this He has created a map that shows where all of the mines are located and how we can avoid them. This map is often referred to as God's commands or God's laws. These commands are summarized in the Ten Commandments that God gave Moses at Mount Sinai during the exodus of the Israelites from Egypt.

Four of these commands are about our relationship with the Creator:
- Have no other Gods, only me.
- Do not make and worship any idols.
- Respect my name and what it stands for.
- Set aside one day of the week to rest and reflect on who I am.

And six cover our relationship with people:
- Honor your father and mother.
- Don't commit murder.
- Don't commit adultery.
- Don't steal.
- Don't tell lies about your neighbor.
- Don't covet what other people have.

At the time that God gave Moses these laws; most of the people did not internalize them because they did not have a personal relationship with God. So it was necessary for the laws to be written down and enforced by threat of punishment. This was the basis of the old covenant that God made with the children of Israel.

Later, the Old Testament prophet, Jeremiah, wrote that God would replace the old covenant with a new one. As part of this new covenant God said, "I will put my laws in their hearts, and I will write them on their minds." God accomplishes this by having His Holy Spirit live in us.

When Jesus was asked what the most important commandment was, He responded by saying: "Love the Lord your God with all your heart and with all your soul and with all your mind; the second is this: Love your neighbor as yourself."Then, Jesus said, "All the law and Prophets hang on these two commandments."

With these comments, Jesus was showing us that God's love in us plays a central role in our knowing right from wrong.

Our vision drives our choices.

Many of us never reach our full potential because of the choices that we make.

It is a broadly accepted fact that where we are in life is mostly the result of all the choices that we have made. Given this reality, it is clear that our choices do have consequences and they do matter.

This principle also applies to Kingdom living because our need to make choices does not go away. In fact, you can make a point that our choices become more difficult because they are no longer just "all about us" - they also impact our relationship with God and our fellow believers.

Unfortunately, many believers live frustrated, unfruitful lives because their choices are not driven by the proactive vision of their role in God's Kingdom. And without a personal vision, their lives become reactive rather than proactive. Their decisions are reactive because they end up trying to live their lives being governed by a set of rules. Eventually, the rules become their "religion," their lives go in circles, and they end up in bondage to the rules. And being in bondage, they don't experience the joy and peace that the angels promised to the shepherds when Jesus was born.

Related information

Have you ever thought about whether you live your life reactively or proactively? If not, you should, because it has a lot to do with how things turn out for you. My observation is that the best that those who live their life reactively achieve is mediocrity. In contrast, the sky is the limit for those who are proactive. These outcomes differ because reactive people are continually reacting to what is happening while proactive people are making things happen.

So, why would you choose to be reactive rather than proactive? Probably because being reactive is a lot less work, requires very little homework, no goals, taking much less risk, and

Why It Matters What You Believe!

> *not having to take responsibility for results. On the other hand, being proactive takes a lot more effort because it requires that you develop a vision (plan), do your research, take risks and possibly fail, and take ownership of results.*
>
> *If this is so, why would you want to live life proactively? Because being proactive is a lot more rewarding and a lot more fun!*

So what is this vision thing? If you have ever set a goal, you have had a vision. In goal setting, we are, in effect, visualizing a future that does not presently exist. In fact, we are doing more than visualizing; we are using all of our five senses - sight, smell, sound, taste, and touch - as well as future gratification, to develop an "emotionally compelling" reason for achieving our goal.

So, how does this work out in real life? Suppose that you establish a goal to bake a chocolate cake from scratch for the family. You visualize the completed cake's appearance, smell its aroma, feel its soft texture, savor its taste, and hear your family raving about how good it tastes. All of these combine to give you an emotionally compelling reason to complete your goal.

The process of preparing the cake takes some time. It includes: developing a plan (recipe), getting the ingredients at the store, measuring and mixing the ingredients, washing the pots and pans, and baking the cake. You may even burn your finger and spill some stuff along the way. This experience teaches something else about having a vision. Our vision makes suffering and disappointment bearable. It also generates hope in the midst of despair and provides courage and endurance in tribulation.

And finally, our vision creates the framework for the choices that are necessary for us to fulfill that vision. The saying, "If you don't know where you are going, any road will get you there," reflects how a life without vision has unconstrained choices. Said another way, for us to achieve our vision requires that we have self control, personal restraint and discipline.

God's purpose drives our God-given vision.

Our vision always proceeds out of our purpose. This may not be evident because most of us are not conscious of the purposes that are driving our lives. We only become aware of them when we find ourselves riding precariously through life's rapids on an out-of-control raft, and we ask ourselves "Why am I here and why am I doing this?"

When we answer that question, we realize that we have adopted the purposes that were suggested to us by our parents, peers (Jones'), teachers, advertisers, Hollywood, or country; without giving it much thought.

In my case, I was 55 years old before I finally thought much about what purposes were driving my life. Economically, I had hit the wall. A development project that I was involved in was not working out financially. I found myself six million dollars in the hole with very little cash.

I hired a business coach to help me assess why I had gotten myself in this situation and what I needed to do to get through it. One day he asked me to describe for him what I envisioned as an optimal successful outcome for my situation. After I described it he said, "You know that's not going to happen." To which I responded, "If that's so, why did you ask me the question?" His answer was profound. He said, "The reason I asked you the question was to show you that you will never accomplish a goal unless you have an emotionally compelling reason driving it; and your emotionally compelling reasons will come from your purpose in life. So for our next meeting, I want you to figure out why you are doing what you are doing."

Suppose someone gave you that assignment. How would you answer? Initially, I drew a blank. I had no clue. I had never thought about it before. In hindsight, the reason I didn't have a clue was because my driving purposes were imbedded in my subconscious mind. That explains why my search led me to think about the feelings and emotions that I experienced from my various business endeavors.

What I discovered when I examined my feelings was that there was a combination of purposes that drove what I was doing. I enjoyed the challenge of taking risks. I enjoyed being a player in the community. I enjoyed creating and coaching an organization. I enjoyed the freedom of running my own show. I enjoyed the game.

I was surprised to find that I was not in it for the money. In fact, the thought of being rich made me uncomfortable.

Clearly, this had to change, because without money, I could not play the game! The banks expected to be paid back. The insurers, who were bonding our work, expected us to be financially viable. Employees and venders expected to be paid, and customers expected to be served.

I also needed to erase the separation that had developed between my walk with God and my business life. To do this, I had to recognize that when I called God, "Lord," I was recognizing that God owned everything. Therefore, I had to be willing to accept the responsibility of being an effective steward of all that God would bless me with.

After I adjusted my purpose, God gave me a clear vision of what needed to be done, and brought the people and resources to me that were needed to make that vision a reality. In the end, what actually happened was better than the optimal outcome I had described to my business coach!

The same principles apply to understanding what's involved in developing our God-given vision. In order for us to develop our God-given vision, we need to adopt God's priority as our purpose. As we said earlier, Jesus' priority is that every person on earth has an opportunity to hear the Good News that Jesus loves them and has provided a way for them to have the free gift of eternal life; and for those who accept that gift to identify with God in His three persons through the act of baptism; and, finally, that they be taught how to live as spiritually reborn citizens of God's Kingdom.

While we can make a conscious decision to adopt God's purpose to be our purpose, that decision will not carry much weight with our subconscious mind unless we are "attached to the vine;" with Jesus living in us and we in Him. That's because we need the Holy Spirit to fully reveal the magnitude of God's love that is behind God's purpose. For it is our awareness of this love that becomes the emotionally compelling reason for our subconscious mind's willingness to buy into adapting God's purpose as its purpose.

The context of our God given vision.

As spiritually reborn citizens of God's Kingdom, we are part of a global community of believers. The Bible refers to us as "brothers and sisters in Christ." We are siblings because the same Holy Spirit lives in each of us and, because of that relationship, our lives exhibit the same "fruits of the Spirit" that we discussed earlier.

The Bible also uses the word picture of a physical body to describe the variety of roles each of us plays as a part of that community. Just like a physical body needs all of its parts (fingers, feet, nose, eyes, digestive system, lungs, etc.) in order to function optimally, the community of believers needs the various gifts that God gives each of us in order to function as well.

When the New Testament was written a little less than 2,000 years ago, one writer listed the gifts that were needed at that time as follows: apostles, prophets, teachers, miracle workers, healers, helpers, organizers, and those who pray in tongues.

Today, given the increase in knowledge and technology, the list could be expanded to include such gifts as councilors, writers, publishers, translators; airplane pilots and technicians; movie and television producers and technicians; actors, musicians, financial supporters, and IT technologists, just to name a few.

So, a good place to begin the quest for our vision will be for us to ask God to identify those gifts that He has given us; how He wants those gifts to be used in serving as Kingdom citizens; and finally, where God wants us to serve.

More than likely, our particular gift will need to be coordinated with other believers' gifts in order to be effective. This means that we will be using our gift within the context of an organization.

The most common organization involving the community of believers is a church. The church is the support group that we need to be a part of in order to have access to the gifting of others, as well as to contribute our gifting to meet the needs of others and carry out God's purpose on earth.

It's also where we have access to the principle of spiritual compounding. Jesus said that, "where two or three believers are meeting because they are mine, I will be there with them, and if two of you agree down here on earth concerning anything you ask for, my Father in Heaven will do it for you."

If acting on your God-given vision seems intimidating, keep in mind that God is not going to ask us to do anything that He hasn't given us the power to do. And further, God, being all knowing, already knows how it is all going to turn out.

This book is a good example of how this works. In my conversations with people I realized that my life's experiences had given me a unique perspective on what a relationship with the Creator should look like. I became convinced that my perspective would be helpful for some people in their decision to believe in Jesus and be spiritually reborn.

My problem was that my formal training was in civil engineering and my life's work was in building businesses. How would I communicate these ideas? God then planted the thought that I needed to write a book that would be easy to read and have the potential for electronic publication around the world. Even if only one percent of the people on the planet were helped by it, that one percent would be sixty million people. Wow! How is that for a God given vision?

My problem was that I had never written a book before. What if I failed and looked foolish? It was then that I realized that this was not about me, it was about Him. He would have to give me the words to write. All I had to do was be willing to do my part. The fact that you are reading this book means that you are now a part of this vision.

PART VIII

The Benefits of Believing God

The Bible gives the believer insight into today's world news.

Did you ever wonder why so much of today's news is about a small country named Israel of which Jerusalem is the capital? After all, this country is only 62 years old and it only has a population of little more than five million of the world's total population of thirteen million Jewish people, on a land mass the size of the state of New Jersey.

The Bible has much to say about present-day Israel and the times we are living in. The prophet, Ezekiel, writing more than 2,500 years ago, foretold that God would disperse the Jews throughout the world, let them endure intense persecution, and eventually He would reestablish His people as a nation in the land we now call Israel. Ezekiel said that the cities would be rebuilt, the nation would prosper, and the land would yield bountiful crops.

Ezekiel also foretold that God would set a trap for a group of nations made up of ancient peoples that resided in the areas we now refer to as Libya, Ethiopia, Iran, Turkey, Syria, Lebanon, the Arab nations, and Russia as their leader. The trap will be sprung when they attack Israel with the goal to destroy the people and gather the plunder. God will step in and destroy eighty-five percent of their armies. Ezekiel wrote that God will do this to show His greatness and bring honor to His name.

The prophet, Daniel, foretold the succession of five major world powers that we now know as Babylonian, Persian, Greek, Roman and one that has not happened yet. The one that is yet to happen is the revived Roman Empire in the form of a ten nation confederation.

A leader will rise and absorb three of these nations and take control of this confederation. The Bible calls this leader the Antichrist because of his and his confederation's satanic inspiration. At the time of Jesus' return to earth to rule from Jerusalem, this person will be the dominant world leader. His control of society will be so complete that he will require all people to pledge their allegiance to him by affixing his symbol on their hand or forehead in order to buy or sell anything. (Note that electronic currency and embedded computer chips have now made this possible.)

The Bible says that this mark is represented by the number 666 and refers to this mark as "the mark of the beast." Those who accept this mark must know that it represents allegiance to Satan because their acceptance of the mark dooms them to eternal damnation.

Earlier, I described how those who are believers would be quietly withdrawn from the earth and transported to Heaven. What do we know about the timing of this event? While on earth, Jesus was asked when it would happen and He indicated that only God knew the exact date. However, Jesus did say that all of the people on the earth would be exposed to the Gospel before it would happen. He also indicated that the generation that saw the reestablishment of Israel would experience the withdrawing of the believers from earth.

These examples are but a small part of all that is foretold in the Bible. This is because approximately twenty-five percent of the book is about prophecies of future events. Some of these prophecies have already taken place, many are taking place during our time, and others will take place in the future.

Biblical prophecy is a reflection of the fact that the Creator knows everything, even future events, and He chooses to reveal

His knowledge of those events so that those of us who believe in Him will have confidence in our future.

Now you know why it really does matter what you believe.

Now that you have read through this overview of what the Bible says about the Creator, as well as His plans and expectations, you probably agree that it really does matter what you believe. As they say in tennis, the ball is now in our court. Sooner or later, we will need to decide what we are going to do with it.

I am reminded of Peter Drucker's response when he was asked why he was a believer. The great business and management thinker said that being a believer made sense because it is such a good deal.

Is it a good deal? Let's examine the consequences of our choosing to believe God:
- We gain eternal life.
- We gain an intimate relationship with the Creator.
- We gain citizenship in the Creator's eternal Kingdom.
- We gain the Creator's Spirit living in us.
- His Spirit makes sure that we are never alone.
- His Spirit teaches us about the Creator.
- His Spirit teaches us about Kingdom living.
- His Spirit confirms the Creator's forgiveness of our rebellion, helping us see ourselves as the Creator sees us.
- His Spirit gives us access to the Creator's love, power, and wisdom.
- His Spirit helps us to see other people from the Creator's perspective.

- His Spirit gives us the power to resist Satan's temptation to do wrong.
- We gain a life that has eternal purpose and significance making it possible for us to live life to our full potential.
- We have the promise that our needs will be met.
- We gain the benefits of being a part of the Creator's global family of believers; giving us access to their love, encouragement, support, wisdom and help in carrying out the vision that the Creator gives us.
- We gain the joy and peace that the angels promised the shepherds the night Jesus was born.

However, you need to know that there is some risk for those who believe the Gospel, particularly if you have grown up and live in a society that is predominantly Muslim. At the very least you will be ostracized by family and friends. In some cases your life may be in danger.

Also, if you live in a society that envisions itself as being a secular humanist utopia on earth - one such as communist Russia and China were in the past - your life would also be in danger. You would have been in danger because the freedom that you have in your spiritually reborn life is a threat to leaders of those tightly controlled countries.

And finally, looking ahead to the time when the earth is ruled by the person that the Bible refers to as the Antichrist; that will be a time when refusing to accept the "Mark of the Beast," mentioned earlier, will lead to almost certain martyrdom.

I mention these extreme cases of risk so you will be aware of the possibility that some people will not feel comfortable with your decision; you will just have to accept that.

A note to my grandchildren and great grandchildren.

You are the primary reason for this book.

One day, a couple years ago, I was thinking of you. I began to wonder what it would be like for us to have a conversation. My thoughts shifted to trying to envision what your world would be like 50 years from now. What would I want you to know?

Then my mind wandered to thinking of my grandparents and great grandparents. It dawned on me that I had benefited from their vision for my generation. While they did not communicate with us directly, they were reborn Christians, lived lives of great faith in God's Word, and prayed often that their children and succeeding generations would eventually join them in Heaven.

Then it occurred to me that the most important thing that I could share with you would be to introduce you to our Creator and tell you about the exciting future He has planned for you. My prayer is that you will accept what Jesus has done for you. And when you get to Heaven, be sure to look me up because I look forward to getting to know you.

ACKNOWLEDGMENTS

It's hard to know where to begin.

I was blessed with my parents, Henry and Elizabeth, who believed the Creator and encouraged each of their eight children to examine the evidence before making their own decision about the existence of the Creator. I thank my soul mate, Mary, for her support and encouragement. Also, I thank my children and grandchildren for giving me a special appreciation for future generations.

For all of you who have contributed to my knowledge on the book's subject - I thank you. These include the writers of the Bible, teachers, and preachers, plus business writers, consultants, and associates that I've read and worked with.

A special thanks to my business associate, Steve Gunlock, who encouraged me to write this book, and to all who read manuscript drafts and provided valuable feedback.

And most important of all, I want to acknowledge the contribution of the Creator's Holy Spirit who dwells in me. Much of the detail, content, and flow of this work are His. I thank Him for using me in this way.